YOUR HOME IS MAKING YOU SICK

How to Create a Healthy Home

EDWARD KAMPF

WWW.SELFPUBLISHN30DAYS.COM

Published by *Self Publish -N- 30 Days*

Printed in the United States of America

ISBN: 9-798-68186-805-7

1. Nonfiction 2. House and Home 3. Cleaning, Caretaking 4. Safety 5. Cleaniness
Edward Kampf *Your House is Making You Sick*

Disclaimer/Warning:

DEDICATION

Thank you to my family and friends for always believing in me.

To all my Superstar Realtor friends,

To my beautiful Z team - Zack and Zoe,

I love you all!

CONTENTS

INTRODUCTION

Your Home Is Making You Sick

Your home should be a sanctuary of health and comfort. This book will provide a roadmap to convert your home into a healthy and happy home.

My journey began after my daughter spent the weekend at a prominent hotel on a religious retreat. Upon pickup, she had a rash on the exposed parts of her body, her arms, and her legs.

After a discussion with a pediatrician, I was told it was Dust Mite poisoning from a toxic environment. A hotel room is a toxic environment?

My research about the toxicity of indoor environments sparked a new passion. I learned about the importance of mattress sanitizing, as well as hazards in our homes; viruses, bacteria, allergens, mold, germs, and the off-gassing of toxic chemicals.

I left a career in mortgage banking and created a company based on the concept of creating healthy homes by treating toxic environments with nontoxic solutions.

Shortly after founding my company, I discovered allergists and breathe center specialists wanted absolutely nothing to do with me. Ironically, one allergist told me I was bad for his business. However, he was interested in having his home treated.

Do you recall an allergist or physician asking (during a health check) about your home's age? Or discussing exposure to toxins? Doctors suggest allergy testing to discover food, mold, and pet allergies, but never quiz about the toxicity of the environment in which we reside.

Pharmacies sell hundreds of prescriptions and allergy medications. However, not one pill solves the root of an allergy sufferer's problem. Drugs mask symptoms to provide temporary relief. Imagine if there was a pill that would permanently solve all allergy and respiratory issues? There probably is one, but we will never hear about it.

After a history of visiting my allergist twice a year (36 years) for temporary relief, it ended as my discovery began.

Disclosure:

I am not a doctor.

I am not an indoor air specialist.

I am not a certified mold remediator.

I am not a certified mold inspector.

I am not an antimicrobial scientist.

I am neither a mycologist nor an entomologist.

I am not an author.

I am simply a former allergy sufferer who decided enough was enough.

BASIC GUIDE

Brief Description

Two words, germs, and bacteria are often interchangeable today. "Germs" is not used widely in the medical community or the scientific community as it used to be. The word "bacteria" is more prominent and acceptable. Germs, however, encompass bacteria, fungi, viruses, and protozoa. The term "germs" can be applied to any of the microscopic particles that can cause illness in humans.

Bacteria are microscopic, single-celled organisms that can live almost anywhere, including water, dirt, air, carpet, and furniture. Microbiology experts estimate there are hundreds of millions of species of bacteria. Most are harmless and can even be beneficial to humans, so you sometimes hear about "good" bacteria versus "bad" bacteria. Many of today's cleaning products have chemicals to kill good bacteria. Experts have argued that killing off good bacteria can even have a negative impact on your health.

There are plenty of bad bacteria that are the cause of a wide range of illnesses. Some of those bacteria cause disease and produce toxins, which are deadly chemicals that damage cells and make people sick. For this reason, keeping bacteria at bay is very important.

A single bacterial cell can multiply to thousands within a few hours.

At room temperature:

After 3 ½ hours, 16,382 cells.
After 4 hours, 65,386 cells.
After 5 hours, 1,048, 576 cells.

Mold begins to grow as soon as its spores land on damp, fiber-rich material (wood, fabric, and drywall), and it can spread around a house within 24-48 hours. It colonizes in one to twelve days and grows one square inch per day.

Volatile organic compounds (VOCs) are organic chemicals with a high vapor pressure at ordinary room temperature. Their high vapor pressure results from a low boiling point, which causes large numbers of molecules to evaporate or sublimate from the liquid or solid form of the compound and enter the surrounding air, a trait known as volatility.

CHAPTER ONE

Sleeping with the Enemy

There is no better place to start than the area of a home where we spend the most amount of quality time: our bed.

Dust Mites are invisible to the naked eye. A female Dust Mite may lay 200 eggs. Where do they live? Well, they need warmth, moisture, and food to flourish: the warmer the environment, the more ideal their breeding ground. Therefore, a mattress provides the perfect nesting place.

Dust Mites are harmless in the sense that they don't bite and only want your exfoliated skin particles. The truth is, we are not allergic to Dust Mites per se, it's their fecal particles that are the root of many health problems, i.e., skin rashes, itchy eyes, migraines, depression, fatigue, and allergies. When ingesting the waste products of Dust Mites, immune systems kick into high gear, producing antibodies against ordinarily harmless substances. This overzealous immune response causes the symptoms associated with a Dust Mite allergy.

The average Mite releases 8-20 fecal particles a day. The average one-year-old mattress contains over 1 million Dust Mites. If you do the math, well, don't do the math. Do you sleep with your mouth open? Dust Mites love to congregate and imbibe the moisture from your breath.

According to several web sources, the average person swallows 52 spiders over the course of a lifetime. Dust Mites belong to the arachnid family, so I would add about a trillion more zeros to that claim.

An article in the Wall Street Journal (WSJ) February 2010 claimed a mattress doubles in weight over ten years due to debris and Dust Mite droppings. A follow-up article claimed there was no evidence to support that. Mattresses take a beating each year, so it's best to replace them every decade as our bone structure shifts as we get older.

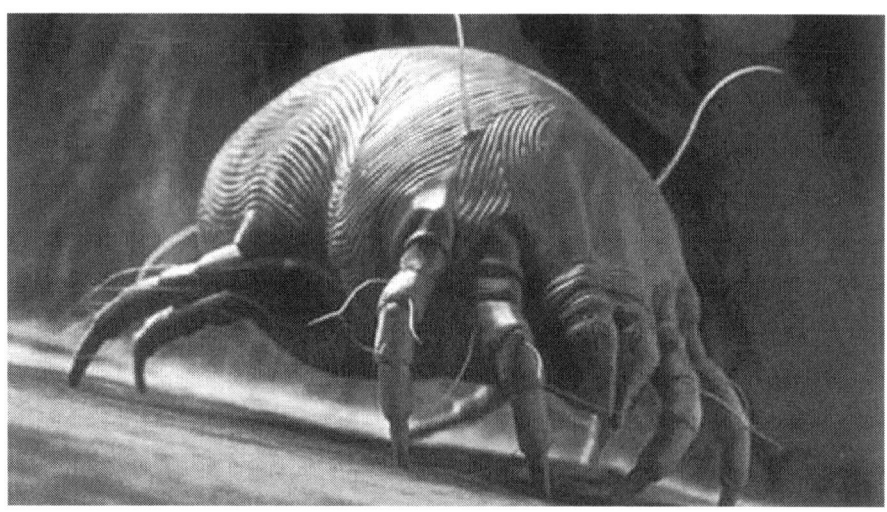

Sanitizing a mattress every three months via an environmentally safe, no water, steam, or chemical process, and you will begin each day well-rested and breathing clearly.

CHAPTER TWO

Don't Let the Bed Bugs Bite

I'd be remiss if I didn't mention Bed Bugs. A female Bed Bug can lay 100 eggs over the course of a month. By the time they are discovered, an infestation of thousands can exist. They are portable and continuously search for new habitats. If one Bed Bug remains after an extermination treatment, be prepared for a sequel.

Dust Mites and Bed Bugs are very different organisms and affect humans in very different ways. Dust Mites are microscopic bugs that primarily live on dead skin cells regularly shed from humans and their pets. They don't carry disease. Bed Bugs, on the other hand, are small wingless insects that are part of the arachnid family that feed solely upon the blood of warm-blooded animals. They pierce the skin with their elongated beak—like a hypodermic needle. Bed Bugs inject their victims with their saliva, which contains a numbing agent, like Novocain. They drink until they become engorged with a person's blood—crawling away satisfied—until the next night. The life span depends on conditions as nymphs can survive prolonged starvation periods—up to a year.

One Bed Bug transported home (usually) from a hotel room will ruin your life for weeks. Exterminators charge a small fortune to saturate a home with toxic chemicals to kill the pests. I prefer the heating technique as heat is clean and does not leave a poisonous chemical footprint. (Bed Bugs die at 130 degrees). Find a reputable exterminator who offers the heating technique as an option.

Check for Bed Bugs immediately upon entering a hotel room. Place luggage on a luggage rack, not the floor. Look in empty drawers and pull bedsheets off the corners of the mattress. Bed Bugs are easy to spot.

CHAPTER THREE

More Reasons Why You Should Sleep Standing Up

A mattress is the most toxic piece of furniture in a home. Bed Bug infestation and Dust Mite poisoning aside, here are additional reasons why you should learn to sleep standing up:

Foam mattresses – Foam is widely used in a mattress because it's cheap to produce. Foam is made from petroleum products containing a "witch's brew" of toxic chemicals. Over time, foam deteriorates, releasing particles into the air where they can be ingested. The particles are called "chemical dust." A polyurethane foam mattress loses half its weight over ten years of use. It begs the question, "Is my bed making me fat, too?"

Because foam is highly flammable, a large number of toxic flame retardants are added. Some fire marshals call foam "Solid Gasoline." As a result, these beds are soaked in the most powerful and dangerous chemical flame retardants.

The most common Chemical Flame Retardants are Antimony, Boric Acid, and Halogenated Flame Retardants (HFRs).

Antimony is a toxic heavy metal that can cause eye, heart, and lung problems.

Boric Acid can cause eye and respiratory irritation.

HFR may be the worst of the bunch. They are linked to severe problems that can span generations:

- Delay puberty and reproductive development and cause neurobehavioral changes
- Disrupt thyroid hormones
- May cause cancer and demonstrated to harm sperm and their mobility, even across two generations
- Harm brain and nerve function

Please sit before reading this next statement.

Mattress companies are not required to disclose their flame retardant chemicals. Mattress companies call their formulation "proprietary," therefore they are as protected as Coca-Cola's formula.

Just a few more side effects from those toxic chemicals:

Mammary tumors, damage to the liver, kidney and central nervous systems, cancer ... but on the happy side, you will never burn to death on your mattress! (Ugh!)

Conventional mattresses are chock full of nasty, toxic chemicals, too, that are linked to a huge list of severe health complications, including SIDS, asthma, allergies, reproductive toxicity, respiratory problems, skin irritation, cancer and more.

A study performed several years ago by the University of Texas on the safety of crib mattresses revealed frightening results (April 6, 2014, *Austin American-Statesman*).

Babies are exposed to chemical emissions from crib mattresses while they sleep.

A team of university environmental engineers analyzed the foam padding and plastic covers of 20 new and old crib mattresses and found they emitted volatile organic compounds similar to those found in lemon-scented sprays and other household items.

The study found that new crib mattresses release four times as many chemicals as older mattresses. Older mattresses have more time to air out, so those UT engineering students were on the right track.

The engineers were interested in studying crib mattresses because of the time babies spend sleeping—50-60 percent of their days. They suggested "airing out" a new crib mattress.

I found the study short-sided and missing a significant mark. Unlike adults who use pillows for elevation, babies sleep with their face directly on the crib mattress. Why didn't they pursue a study linking Sudden Infant Death Syndrome to the volatile organic compounds toxins or the toxic chemicals from flame retardant chemicals? I honestly do not know how crib mattress manufacturer's sleep at night -- certainly not like a baby!

Suggestions:

When purchasing a new crib mattress, let it bake in the hot sun for a day or so. The natural antimicrobials from the sun will sanitize, while toxic chemicals are diluted by off-gassing.

Hand-me-down crib mattresses should be sprayed with an environmentally safe antibacterial solution and aired out for safety as well. (Babies, eat, sleep, and what?)

When purchasing a new mattress, leaving it outside is not an option, especially if it's a queen or king. Have a professional mattress sanitizing company use a UV-C germicidal light to sanitize it. These processes will off-gas the toxic chemicals and create long-term health and life to your mattress.

CHAPTER FOUR

Your Shower Curtain is Killing You

Yes, your shower curtain is hazardous to our health. ***Don't believe me?*** Ask Janet Leigh.

Here are 10 cancer-causing products you should be aware of and remove from your home:

1. Air Fresheners—The vast majority of commonly known air fresheners, even some marked "all-natural" or "unscented," contain compounds called phthalates. Different types of phthalates have different health consequences. A majority of them affect reproductive health. Once these chemicals enter the bloodstream, they can alter hormone levels and cause other health issues. One medical journal (*Journal of Environmental Health Perspectives*) linked it to breast cancer. Another medical report suggested phthalates promotes prostate cancer proliferation.

   One popular brand contains over 80 known toxic chemicals, including Genotoxins, Bronchoconstrictors, Neurotoxins, Reproductive Toxins, Hepatotoxins, and Mutagenic Chemicals. (I prefer not to mention which deodorizer because I don't want to be sued by Febreze.)

   Plug-In deodorizers contain over 3,000 chemicals that suck oxygen from a room. Place a house plant next to a plug-in deodorizer, and it will suffocate and die.

   Another hazard occurs when the oil depletes. They can reach over 180 degrees and potentially cause a fire.

   Homemade air fresheners are the simplest products to make: distilled water with a few drops of your favorite essential oil.

2. Candles – Particles from burning candles are extremely dangerous. Some have a stronger effect than diesel exhaust particles.

   Exposure to particles from burning candles can shorten your life. A scientific study on mice found that exposure to particles from burning candles significantly increased the progression of clogged arteries, increasing the likelihood of heart attacks, stroke, and even death.

Although the US Consumer Council banned the sale of candles containing lead wicks, it is still a good idea to make sure they don't have this potentially dangerous substance.

A simple way to check is to use a piece of paper. Holding the wick, try to draw a line on paper. If there is no line, then the wick most likely does not contain lead. You can also light the candle and hold the paper high above the flame. If a gray soot residue forms, your candle may have lead.

Everyone loves candles, so buy smart. Read labels and purchase in stores that care about our earth.

3. Shower Curtain—Did you young folks Google Janet Leigh? Thanks to her (and Hitchcock), millions of people checked behind their shower curtain before using their restroom. Some still do!

You may recognize the term PVC. PVC is the third highest produced type of plastic in the world. Though it's safe for transporting water and sewer in pipes throughout your home, PVC products are a ticking time bomb in your home. Polyvinyl Chloride is the non-abbreviated name.

It's not only in your shower curtain and liner. It can be found in children's toys, containers, and other plastic objects. When PVC is used in closed environments, it releases toxic carcinogenic compounds.

Okay, I know, you need a shower curtain, and the kids will scream if you chunk their toys, so I suggest aerating any plastic object brought into your home. That includes all electronics. (TVs, computers). Set them outside for a few hours to off-gas.

4. Carpet Cleaners and Fabric Shampoos – Many of the cleaners contain stain removal components. One component is perchloroethylene. Perchloroethylene, also called Tetrachlorethylene, has been linked to increased risks of developing lung cancer. Carpet cleaners and fabric shampoos also contain a compound called naphthalene. Naphthalene is the main ingredient in mothballs. Exposure is linked to throat and lung cancer.

Baking soda is a great odor remover, and white vinegar is effective for removing dirt stains.

Steam cleaning is another healthy option for keeping carpets clean, providing the carpet cleaner avoids harsh chemicals and fragrances.

Another study found that hardwood floors were a better option. Not so fast, Cowboy! More on laminate floors, later.

5. Dry Cleaning Products – According to the American Cancer Society, another carcinogen hidden in your home could be Tetrachlorethylene or Perchlorethylene that is commonly used in dry cleaning. These chemicals are often included as solvents in dry cleaning products.

Wearing clothes that were dry-cleaned can unintentionally expose you to these harmful substances. Make sure your preferred cleaner does not use perchloroethylene.

6. Insecticides and Pesticides – Sadly, many of the pet-friendly solutions are not human friendly. A number of the tick, flea and lice control products have potentially carcinogenic chemicals.

Some list organophosphate insecticides. Very toxic!

7. Antibacterial Products – Just the name alone makes you think it's safe, right? They are designed to make our environment

safer, however recent concerns led to the banning of triclosan. Triclosan is an antibacterial and antifungal ingredient found in many cosmetics, soaps, detergents, and toothpaste (Colgate).

Initial tests on mice caused enough concern to ban the product.

Products like silver have been used for their antibacterial and antimicrobial properties. The use of silver does not seem to pose any significant danger to humans.

There are several antibacterial products that are EPA/FDA approved/registered. Reoccurring theme: READ LABELS!

8. Deodorants – There are numerous claims that deodorants could be harmful and cause cancer. The editor-in-chief of *The Journal of Applied Toxicology* claims that wiping the chemicals found in deodorants under your arms and on the sides of your chest or breasts "could provide a route of almost direct exposure to underlying tissue containing estrogen receptors." This is concerning because, both parabens and aluminum, found in deodorants, are "estrogenic" chemicals – which means they interact with your body's cells in ways similar to estrogen. According to the National Cancer Institute, estrogen plays a huge role in promoting the growth of cancer cells, which is a significant concern because of the daily exposure to deodorants. "They significantly add to estrogen burdens."

Buy deodorants with only naturally-derived ingredients: no aluminum, artificial fragrance, or artificial preservatives.

9. Toothpastes containing triclosan – Colgate-Palmolive Co. has been using triclosan since its approval by the FDA in 1997. Colgate Total has provoked a lot of debate. Let's end it now.

Though you don't usually swallow or ingest toothpaste, ingredients are still absorbed through soft tissues of the mouth and can enter your bloodstream.

A. Fluoride—Though fluoride prevents cavities, tooth decay and can prevent cavities, when too much fluoride is ingested, it can lead to fluoride toxicity, which causes rashes, stomach pain, headaches, and vomiting.

B. Titanium Dioxide—This inorganic compound gives toothpaste its pleasant bright, white color. Titanium dioxide nanoparticles can penetrate your gums and have toxic reactions in your brain and cause nerve damage.

C. Sodium Lauryl Sulfate – This surfactant or foaming agent is often derived from coconut or palm kernel oil but is contaminated with toxic by-products during the manufacturing process.

D. Carrageenan – Extracted from red seaweeds, this substance is used for thickening and stabilizing properties. It has no nutritional value and shouldn't be consumed regularly.

Seek toothpastes that are free of Lauryl Sulfates, Saccharin, and Propylene Glycol as well.

10. Aluminum foil – Basically, wrapping hot food in foil or using it to bake isn't all that safe. Think about it. Your food is coming in direct contact with a form of metal and, at certain temperatures, will cause the aluminum to leach into the food.

Many studies have linked the increase of aluminum foil in our everyday lives to the rising cases of male infertility.

It has also been known to cause loss of coordination and Alzheimer's.

Use glass containers for baking and food storage to cut exposure.

Non-Stick Pans – Layers of chemical coating eliminate sticking. When heated, they can release those harmful chemical and toxic gasses into the air. Not only does your food become laced, but you're inhaling it as well.

The best alternative is a cast-iron skillet.

Bonus since you read this far …

10.1   Miscellaneous Plastics – There are many types of plastic with all different levels of toxicity. These are the worst:

BPA stands for bisphenol A. BPA is an industrial chemical that has been used to make certain plastic and resins since the 1960s. BPA is found in polycarbonate plastics and epoxy resins.

Polycarbonate plastics are often used in containers that store food and beverages, such as water bottles. They may also be used in consumer goods.

Exposure to BPA is a concern because of possible health effects in the brain and prostate glands of fetuses, infants, and children. It also affects children's behavior.

So, what good is BPA, and why is it used? BPA extends life and protects food from contamination and spoilage.

CHAPTER FIVE

What is Blue and Smells Like Green Paint?

Everything is about sight and smell. A foul odor is the result of a bacterial gas-off. All homes have a distinctive aroma, none of which is natural, so follow your nose.

Indoor Air – Indoor Air Quality (IAQ) is known to affect health, comfort, and well-being of home/building occupants. The EPA coined the terms "Toxic Home Syndrome" and "Sick Building Syndrome."

IAQ can be affected by gases, including carbon monoxide, radon, volatile organic compounds, particulates, microbial contaminants, mold, bacteria, or any mass or energy stressor that can induce adverse health conditions.

According to OSHA (Occupational Safety & Health Administration), humidity in your home can be controlled by maintaining your thermostat between 68-76%.

Contributing factors to toxic home syndrome:

Carbon Monoxide – Inappropriate levels of exhaust—gas stoves, leaking chimney, and furnace.

Carbon Dioxide – By-product of fossil fuel—potential ventilation issue.

Hydrogen Sulfide – Rotten egg smell caused by sewer line leak.

VOC's – Chemicals in building materials that off-gas (more later).

Particulate Matter – Organic and inorganic substance, pest droppings, Dust Mites, pet dander, mold, dirt, etc.

Air filters – The integral role of an air filter is to ensure that the air produced from the HVAC system is free of dust particles and other contaminants that can cause allergies. The best air filters are the least expensive ones that should be replaced every 30 days.

Smoke Detector – All homes should have detectors in each bedroom. They save lives.

Carbon Monoxide Detector – Carbon is an odorless gas that is toxic to ingest. Unfortunately, you won't know if there is a leak and never will, if you know what I mean. Homes with gas water heaters, stoves, etc. should have this detector.

Air Quality Test – All homes should have an air quality test performed every year or every few years. It's best to discover a mold issue early.

What is blue and smells like green paint? Blue paint.

CHAPTER SIX

Breaking the Mold

There are more than 10,000 species of mold living in North American homes, according to the Center for Disease Control (CDC) estimates. The mold that grows inside an enclosed space, such as a house, is different than mold that grows outdoors. Even more astounding is that mold which grows on wood may not be a mold that can grow on fabric. That's because each species of mold likes a specific set of conditions to grow.

Mold is a member of the fungi kingdom. Though there are thousands of strains of mold, most strains belong to one of these five types:

1. Alternaria grows on walls, showers, around windows, under sinks, and in various damp places. It is often found where water damage has occurred. Alternaria mold can appear black, grey, or dark brown and has a wooly texture. Prolonged exposure to these fungi can cause allergic and asthma attacks.

2. Aspergillus is the most common type of mold found indoors. It can look grey, brown, yellow, green, white, or black. Aspergillus mold usually grows on walls, insulation, paper products, and clothing.

   It causes allergic reactions, respiratory infections, as well as inflammation of lungs in people with weak immune systems.

3. Cladosporium can grow in cool areas (unlike many other molds). It usually appears on fabrics, such as carpets or curtains, and wood surfaces, like cabinetry and floorboards.

   It has a characteristic black, grey, or olive-green color. It can cause a variety of respiratory problems.

4. Penicillium can be found on various materials that have been in contact with water, including carpeting, wallpaper, insulation, and mattresses. It looks blue or green and produces healthy,

musty odors. Penicillium spores spread very quickly and often result in allergic reactions.

5. Stachybotrys is often referred to as "black mold" because of its color. It is the most dangerous kind of household mold. The toxic black mold has a characteristic musty odor. Usually, it grows in areas that are consistently damp—around leaky pipes, inside air conditioning ducts where a lot of condensation exists.

   It produces toxic compounds called mycotoxins that can cause severe health problems, such as allergic symptoms, breathing problems, asthma attacks, chronic sinus infections, fatigue, and depression.

A Harvard study claims that roughly 50% of homes in America have some type of mold present. I'll go on record and claim 100% of homes have mold. Mold can be found in every bathroom in America where lengthy hot showers exceed ventilation capability. Remember, when cold air meets warm air, condensation exists. Where you have condensation, you will find mold.

Favorable conditions for mold:

- Roughly 50% or higher humidity
- Damp, dusty condition—clothes
- Stagnant air, in an overly "tight" energy-efficient home

Unfavorable Conditions:

- Adequate ventilation
- Less than 50% humidity

For Real Estate Professionals:
You don't have to become a mold expert. To reduce personal liability, consider the following points during visual inspections:

Pay specific attention to stains or discoloration on ceilings and walls. Big mold problems start with small red flags. Learn to pick up on the red flags associated with plumbing leaks and drainage problems.

If you notice signs of potential mold problems, avoid using terms like "black mold" or "toxic mold." Generic descriptions such as "mold type" or "mildew-like" might be better used.

Always defer to a licensed mold inspector to determine a potential issue.

CHAPTER SEVEN

New Construction, New Destruction

The smell emitted from a newly constructed home is a combination of toxic chemicals released in the air. That emission is called *"off-gassing."* The poisonous chemicals are Volatile Organic Compounds (VOC's).

Over 10,000 chemicals are classified as VOCs. They are easily vaporized and remain in the air (off-gassing). The off-gassing process takes between 2-8 weeks, depending on ventilation.

This is part of the reason the Environmental Protection Agency (EPA) says that indoor air can be two to five (and even up to 200 times) more polluted than outdoor air.

Here are five home construction materials that pose the highest health risk:

1. Carpeting – Almost all carpeting in the United States (the wall-to-wall type) is made of synthetic materials that off-gas toxins such as petroleum by-products and synthetics (polypropylene, nylon, acrylic).

   Soil and stain repellents, vinyl or latex, PVC, urethane, anti-static sprays, artificial dyes, antimicrobial treatments

   Some of these "ingredients" have been linked to cancer, while others may cause nerve damage, respiratory problems, thyroid damage, and damage to the immune system and brain development.

   A baby crawling on a brand-new carpet is equivalent to that baby ingesting four cigarettes a day of pollution, most of which is formaldehyde (EPA). Surprisingly, it is also found in Febreze air freshener. (Oops, poked the Febreze bear again!)

2. Engineered Wood Products – Engineered wood is made by gluing together layers of fragmented wood. It may be used for cabinets, furniture, wall paneling, kitchen counters, and more, but

the adhesives and bonding agents it contains emit pollutants, including formaldehyde, into the air (off-gassing).

A very prominent flooring company recently resolved a $36 million payout on lawsuits over its Chinese laminate flooring. CBS News aired a 60 Minutes investigation into countless class action claims and found 150 boxes of laminate flooring tested over 20 times over the permissible level of formaldehyde set by California law.

Using natural, solid wood for furniture, cabinets, and other indoor wood products can eliminate this problem. There are also engineered wood products developed that contain no or reduced levels of chemicals.

3. Oil-Based Paint, Wood Finishes, and Paint Strippers – Oil-based paints and stains contain potentially 300 toxic chemicals and 150 carcinogens, according to a John Hopkins University study. Among them are alkyl resin, kerosene, lead, lithopone, mercury, methylene chloride, methyl ethyl ketone, mineral spirits, toluene, trichloroethane, and xylene.

Paint strippers required to remove oil-based paint (and to clean brushes) also contain toxic and highly volatile chemicals such as methylene chloride, toluene, acetone, and methanol.

Vapors from oil-based paints and strippers accumulate in the air while painting and can irritate eyes, skin, and lungs.

Synthetic latex is made from two petroleum-based compounds, styrene, and butadiene. Both of these are VOCs and can seriously harm humans.

These include effects on the central nervous system, hearing loss, peripheral neuropathy, an increased risk of leukemia and lymphoma, headache, fatigue, weakness, and depression.

A much safer alternative would be 100% natural latex water-based paints and low-volatility paints, which have fewer toxic solvents. Water-based paint strippers are also available, and though they can still cause eye irritation, they are less harmful.

4. Pressure-treated Wood and Wood Preservatives – Wood preservatives are used to protect the wood from fungi, bacteria, and parasites. It can either be applied to the wood's surface or injected into the wood, in which case it's called "pressure-treated" wood. Wood preservatives include toxic pesticides, creosote, arsenic, and more.

Most treated wood used for residential homes (decks, playgrounds, etc.) contain a mixture of copper, chromium arsenic called chromated copper arsenate, or CCA. Studies have found that the chemicals leach into the ground and transfer to the skin from everyday contact.

This is particularly dangerous for children, who may play on treated-wood playgrounds or decks, then put their hands (which may be contaminated with arsenic or other chemicals) in their mouths.

There are many alternatives to highly toxic pressure-treated wood. Sometimes, wood preservatives are unnecessary, as wood can keep quite well if well-ventilated and kept away from the soil. Hardier woods that are weather-resistant include cedar, redwood, and cypress.

If you must use treated wood, certain varieties contain fewer toxic chemicals than others. Arsenic-free pressure-treated wood is a better alternative.

5. Insulation—Most people are aware of the dangers of asbestos in insulation, but even standard fiberglass can be toxic if inhaled

(some have compared their dangers to those of asbestos), and many varieties also contain formaldehyde that can be released into the air.

Safer types of insulation purchased from green building suppliers, such as cotton insulation or insulation made from recycled paper that is formaldehyde-free, can be installed without using a respirator.

6. Formaldehyde – A known carcinogen found in almost every construction building material, used as a preservative. Formaldehyde is a colorless pungent gas in solutions made by oxidizing methanol.

Symptoms of formaldehyde poisoning:

- Irritation of the eyes, nose, and the throat
- Stuffy or runny nose
- Headache
- Sore Throat
- Tightness in the chest
- Skin rash
- Difficulty in breathing
- Wheezing
- Burnt stomach and burnt esophagus (when formaldehyde is ingested)
- Frequent and severe asthma attacks
- Bronchitis
- Pneumonia
- Restlessness
- Hypotension (in severe cases)
- Arrhythmia (severe poisoning)

- Irregular breathing (in severe cases)
- Loss of consciousness (severe poisoning)

New construction is extremely toxic to a homeowner. Toxic chemicals in construction material require off-gassing before occupancy.

There is a process to off-gas a home removing all toxicity within 24 hours. A complete decontamination process will diminish VOCs within 24 hours (see chlorine dioxide).

CHAPTER EIGHT

Please Be Wise, Sanitize

Yes, there are instructions on the back label of disinfectants. Please read! Not all disinfectants are created equal. Being EPA approved does not mean the solution is nontoxic. (Keep away from children.) Most have a shelf life of 12 months and require a "dwell" time of 10 minutes. Simply spraying and wiping is ineffective in disinfecting or decontamination.

There is a difference between disinfecting and decontamination; DISINFECTING – The removal of MOST contaminants.

DECONTAMINATING – The removal of ALL contaminants.

Most cleaning companies use the term "disinfect" for legal reasons.

A bacterial virus sitting dormant on a surface is called "biofilm." The strength of the disinfectant will determine the "dwell" time of effectiveness in destroying the protein of the biofilm. Reading the back label of a disinfectant will determine the strength of the chemical. Dwell times vary on different products, from 60 seconds to 10 minutes. Most disinfectants promote 10 minutes of dwell time. Again, spraying and wiping is NOT disinfecting. Again, disinfecting is not decontaminating.

Antibacterial

An antibacterial is an agent that inhibits bacterial growth and kills bacteria. Antibacterial solutions are found in soaps, laundry detergents, hand sanitizers, deodorants, and foot powders.

Disinfecting your home with natural, nontoxic cleaners may sound overwhelming, but it's surprisingly simple.

6 Things That Are Naturally Antibacterial That Safely Disinfect

1. White vinegar is a powerful cleaner that easily removes mildew, odors, stains, and wax build-up. Vinegar was found to reduce the

amount of bacteria on a hard surface, though it was less effective than commercial cleaners.

2. Vodka is 80 proof, or 40% alcohol by volume. Like vinegar, vodka degreases, removes stains, shines fixtures, and refreshes fabric—however, there may be a lingering odor.

3. The citrus acid in lemons works amazingly on alkaline stains like soap scum found in bathrooms and kitchens. Lemons can be used to sanitize non-porous surfaces and shine oxidized metals. In the same study, lemons worked to reduce bacteria, however less than vinegar and commercial cleaners.

4. Essential Oils are not only versatile and great smelling. They offer a wide range of medicinal and healing properties. They are quite effective against bacteria and fungus. When added to vodka and/or a soap solution and water, some essential oils can enhance cleaning properties, helping rid your home of mold, mildew, and musty smells.

5. Steam—The simple combination of water and heat produces steam. Steam is the ultimate chemical-free disinfectant.

6. Castile Soap, named after the region in Spain, was once made from olive oil and a blend of vegetable oils. It isn't an antibacterial on its own. However, if you add tea tree essential oil, it will make an effective cleaner.

There are many antibacterial solutions available on grocery store shelves. Find "green" solutions and follow the direction.

Anti-Microbial

Anti-bacterial + antifungal = Antimicrobial

An antimicrobial is an agent that destroys microorganisms or stops their growth. The main class of antimicrobial agents is disinfectants that kill a wide range of microbes on non-living surfaces to prevent the spread of illness.

The active ingredients in antimicrobial technology are:

Silver ion antimicrobials – suitable for a wide range of materials and applications, including medical coatings, plastics, and food-contact products.

Zinc antimicrobials – a broad-spectrum antimicrobial that is commonly favored for its antifungal properties.

Copper antimicrobials – often used as a preservative and are popular for medical products and services.

Antimicrobial technologies can also consist of organic active ingredients such as Quaternary Ammonium Compounds.

An antimicrobial protective shield is created; however, to be most effective, the surface or environment should be treated by an antibacterial for decontamination.

When an inaccurate application is applied with an incorrect dosage, the antimicrobial product is less likely to clean it. Any surviving protein could develop a resistance to the agent, thus creating a "superbug." That unintended consequence creates more long term issues. New superbugs are discovered every day.

Many antimicrobial companies have been created within the past decade. Some claim to keep an environment germ, bacteria, mold, and virus-free for 30, 60, 90 days. To prove the efficacy of effective protection, germ testing must be performed.

On high touch objects such as door handles, light switches, and desktops, friction will wear the protective shield within days. On low or no touch areas such as walls and inner walls where applied, the protective shield could last indefinitely.

Antibacterial and antimicrobial treatments should be performed in every environment where cross-contamination exists, such as day-cares, hospitals, retirement homes, play areas in restaurants, kitchens, office buildings, etc. All public spaces.

Antimicrobial protection can rid the world of so many illnesses and diseases. And it is 100% safe.

CHAPTER NINE

Other Disinfectants and Decontaminators

Ozone Machines – Disclosure: I am 100% against ozone machines. While they are adequate for disinfecting, they are inadequate in destroying viruses and biofilm on surfaces. How is that disinfecting?

They are banned in California and areas of Canada.

They are dangerous and deadly to people, plants, and animals.

Ozone treatments do not destroy mold spores. When used for mold treatment, musty odors always return. When used for odor removal, odors eventually return.

Ozone damages everything electrical: TVs, wall plugs, lighting, appliances, smoke detectors. They corrode rubber washers in sinks, showers and toilets, washing machines, dryers, dishwashers, plastics, leather, and suede.

They are bad for the environment and bad in every environment.

Germicidal UV-C lights – There are three grades of Ultraviolet light:

- UVC—shortest of all UV rays - never reaches the earth because the ozone absorbs it.
- UVB – shortwave, damages skin.
- UVA – long wave—used in tanning beds – may cause skin cancer.

UVC-germicidal light is a high-grade disinfectant, faster than the speed of light. One quick pass will destroy all pathogens and microorganisms.

Used in many hospitals, it does leave a radiation footprint that will dissipate after 5-20 minutes, depending on the usage.

It can cause cancer on extended contact with skin, and eye exposure to the light could cause blindness and/or cataracts.

Bleach—good for discoloring clothes. Does not destroy mold. Every household has a bottle under their kitchen sink. Sorry Clorox, not mine!

DO NOT MIX BLEACH WITH AMMONIA!

Hydrogen Peroxide – a natural disinfectant. Common in many kinds of toothpaste (Chapter 4 #9).

Chlorine Dioxide (clo2) – the strongest oxidizer on this planet. Used during almost every disaster to effectively destroy mold, viruses, bacteria, germs, odors, allergens, and microorganisms. Not to be confused with Chlorine Bleach (Chapter 11).

To accurately prove the effectiveness of any type of sanitizing, testing must be performed:

ATP (adenosine triphosphate) Monitoring is a rapid testing method that quickly assesses the cleanliness of surfaces. Since germs can be transported within a structure, multiple locations inside a home are swabbed to determine to what level an affected area is clean.

ATP bioluminescence testing is a way for us to quickly determine the number of organisms present by detecting ATP. This can be found by measuring the light produced through ATP's reaction with luciferase, a natural firefly enzyme. The more light that is made by using the luminometer is indicative of the quantity of ATP in the sample. While this science is continually expanding into new fields, this type of biologic testing has existed for 50 years.

CHAPTER TEN

The Nose Knows

Odors are the result of a process called off-gassing. The off-gassing process starts with malodorous (foul-smelling) molecules released by any number of sources. While you may try to use deodorizers, air fresheners, or ozone treatments, these products only mask the odors and do nothing to eliminate them permanently. Odor molecules have a secret, migrant life about which most people are unaware.

Once these malodorous molecules are released from the original odor source, they take over the space. These particles invade and inhabit every single porous material imaginable. From drapes to vents, carpets to sub-floors, paint to sheetrock and even studs (and you're not about to replace those!), no porous matter goes untouched, and most surfaces are porous except for glass, porcelain, some countertops. The worst part is that it is only the beginning! The technology behind the science of Chlorine Dioxide in a smoke form consists of releasing odor-destroying molecules that permeate all the porous materials in search of the malodorous molecules everywhere they have permeated (walls, ceilings, cupboards, doors, sub-flooring, studs, etc.). This process destroys the malodorous molecules on a nanoscale. The entire odor cycle is eliminated permanently. There are no toxins, perfumes, or residues of any type.

CHAPTER ELEVEN

Chlorine Dioxide vs. Chlorine Bleach

U nfortunately, the word "chlorine" is found in both Chlorine Dioxide (Clo2) and Chlorine Bleach (NaCIO). This has led to a lot of confusion.

Chlorine bleach is corrosive, toxic, and is weak in destroying bacteria, virus, protozoa, algae, and fungus (mold). Ineffective with killing mold spores.

Bleach releases harmful hypochlorous acid and free chlorine. It's very toxic when mixed with ammonia.

Chlorine Dioxide does not release free chlorine or any harmful by-products.

It's highly effective in eradicating bacteria, viruses, protozoa, algae, and fungus.

It's non-corrosive and does not react with ammonia.

It kills over 35 viruses. To date, no organism tested against chlorine dioxide has proven resistant (including COVID-19).

When used in a gas form, size matters. Over 80,000 clo2 molecules are equivalent to mold or pollen spore.

CHAPTER TWELVE

Quick Guide: How to Maintain a Healthy Home

KEEP IT DRY – Water penetration is the #1 cause of mold. Roof leaks, plumbing issues, and condensation around windows and air ducts are a breeding ground for mold.

KEEP IT CLEAN – Dirt, dust, bacteria should be controlled with regular air filter replacement and vacuums with HEPA airbag.

KEEP IT SAFE – Don't leave harsh chemicals, prescriptions, knives, and firearms accessible to children.

KEEP IT WELL VENTILATED – Indoor air is 200 times more polluted than outdoor air. All electronics, paint, carpet, plastics, etc. produce off-gas. Many regular household items are produced with toxic chemicals. Keep your home well ventilated.

KEEP IT PEST FREE – Bugs leave fecal matter. Keep them out using environmentally safe solutions.

KEEP IT CONTAMINANT FREE – Many household cleaners leave a chemical footprint. Seek environmentally safe "green" products.

KEEP IT MAINTAINED – An organized home is easier to clean than a disorganized home. Make your bed!

KEEP IT THERMALLY CONTROLLED – Condensation forms when warm air meets cool air. Condensation and humidity produce mold. Keep your thermostat regulated. Paying a few extra dollars a month is less expensive than mold remediation.

CHAPTER THIRTEEN

It's Gotten Out of Hand

Anything placed on your skin will enter your bloodstream within 26 seconds—lotions, deodorant, cologne, sunscreen, makeup, etc.

The US Food and Drug Administration (USDA) banned triclosan in hand sanitizers in 2016.

Before the COVID-19 pandemic, mostly obsessed germophobes frequently used hand sanitizers. Today, everyone is obsessed and applying it several times an hour.

Squirt, feel the cool sensation, spread, then feel clean. Easy stuff!

Alcohol, water, fragrance, and glycerin, what could go wrong?

Here are three hidden dangers of hand sanitizers;

1. Antibiotic Resistance: Antibiotics are effective against bacteria. Using hand sanitizers may lower your resistance to antibiotics and, in turn, promote resistance to bacteria.
2. Alcohol Poisoning: Most virus-destroying hand sanitizers are over 70% alcohol. A few squirts of hand sanitizer could equal a couple of shots of hard liquor. School-age kids have been found to consume it.
3. Toxic Chemical: Synthetic fragrances contain phthalates, which are endocrine disruptors and could alter genital development. If the sanitizer is scented, then it's likely to be loaded with toxic chemicals.

Two hand sanitizers I fully endorse.

Germfree 24 – It's an antimicrobial hand sanitizer that lasts 24 hours. It forms an antimicrobial barrier on the skin that will not wash off. It can only be removed by natural exfoliation.

Most hand sanitizers only work when wet, Germfree 24 goes into effect once it's dry.

Rather than killing bacteria by poisoning, it creates a hostile barrier that punctures (like a bed of nails) on contact.

BAC Hand Sanitizer – If you are seeking a hand sanitizer that is 100% plant and mineral-based, PreVasive USA developed an organically-grown sanitizer.

Ingredients: Organic thyme, lemon, and wintergreen oil, 75% (Food Grade) IPA Isopropyl Alcohol from plants.

Non-corrosive, non-staining, highly renewable, and biodegradable, made in the USA.

Nontoxic, non-irritating. GMO-free.

Links to both are available.

CHAPTER FOURTEEN

Hire a Professional

COVID-19 has raised the need for and awareness of disinfecting and decontamination to epic levels.

Famed (deceased) firefighter Red Adair once said, "If you think it's expensive to hire a professional to do a job, wait until you hire an amateur."

Many companies have recently jumped into the disinfecting business. Professional disinfecting/decontamination companies follow a sanitizing protocol. For example:

The first step of any decontamination/deodorizing or sanitizing is to remove the gross contaminants (biofilm).

The strength of the disinfectant will determine if "step one" is performed correctly. Remember, "dwell time."

Back to Red Adair's quote ... the most expensive company is not necessarily the best or most professional. Companies charge by the hour or square foot. Thanks to foggers and electrostatic sprayers, pricing should be fair. An office space of 50,000 square feet can be treated within an hour, depending on the layout and contents.

Within the past 30 days of writing this book, I quoted a business one-tenth of what another company quoted. I took into consideration job time and the fact that they might need re-treatment. Three days after my service, as predicted, they required re-treatment after another employee tested COVID positive.

The COVID-19 pandemic is a humanitarian crisis. This isn't like a catastrophe after a hurricane when only some are affected. We are all affected physically, emotionally, and economically.

I feel very blessed to be in a position where I can help those in need. Unfortunately, this pandemic and perhaps others will be our new normal.

Now, more than ever, it is essential to maintain good health and increase awareness on how to stay healthy in our homes during quarantine and non-quarantine times.

I hope that this book helps in your awareness.

Thank you so much, and let me know how I can help you!

Edward Kampf

Hygienitech Solutions, LLC

713-298-1449

ed@hygienitechsolutions.com

www.hygienitechsolutions.com

Realtors; Please contact me for my TREC approved 2 hour CE class, "Staying Healthy in an Unhealthy Environment."

CHAPTER FIFTEEN

Suggested Links

www.hygienitechsolutions.com complete decontamination/odor & mold removal/ treatment

www.dustfreemattress.com professional mattress sanitizing service

https://www.prevasive.com/pre/ed.kampf organic hand sanitizer

www.zoonousa.com antimicrobial solutions and 24 hour hand sanitizer

www.earthpatriot.com learn about Redox

www.themadoptimist.com amazing soaps- vegan, cruelty-free

www.coxroxconsulting.com Heather Cox – front cover and flyers

APPENDIX

CHLORINE DIOXIDE
GAS SIZE CHART

WHEN IT COME TO CHLORINE DIOXIDE GAS PENETRATION SIZE MATTERS

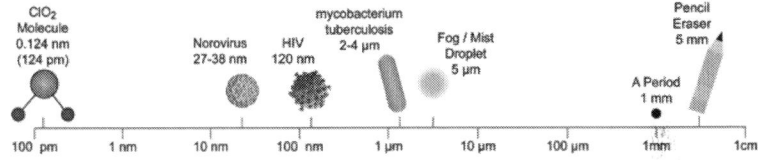

- CHLORINE DIOXIDE GAS MOLECULE SIZE = 0.124 NANOMETERS OR 8.06451612903
- CHLORINE DIOXIDE GAS MOLECULES = 1 NANOMETER
- 1000 NANOMETERS = 1 MICRON

	# OF MICRONS IN SIZE	APPROXIMATE # OF MOLECULES OF CHLORINE DIOXIDE GAS EQUAL TO SIZE OF POLLUTANT
OXYGEN	0.0005	4
ATMOSPHERIC DUST	.001 - 40	8
VIRUSES	.005 - .03	40
TOBACCO SMOKE	.01 - 4	80
OZONE	.01 - .02	800
LEAD	.01 - 0.7	800
BACTERIA	0.3 - 60	2,400
INSECTICIDE DUSTS	0.5 - 10	4,000
PET DANDER	0.5 - 100	4,000
ANTHRAX	1 - 5	8,000
MOLD SPORES	10 - 30	80,000
POLLEN	10 - 1000	80,000

As you can see from the examples above, Chlorine Dioxide Gas can penetrate much deeper into indoor materials, than most toxins, pollen's, viruses or bacteria. This is why Chlorine Dioxide Gas works so well at eliminating indoor odors, reducing indoor allergens, destroying indoor viruses and bacteria.

HYGIENITECH
SOLUTIONS

ed@hygienitechsolutions.com
713.298.1449

hygienitechsolutions.com

HYGIENITECH
S O L U T I O N S

CERTIFICATE OF COMPLETION
COMPLETE DECONTAMINATION & SANITIZATION SERVICE

EPA PRODUCT USED: CHLORINE DIOXIDE

DATE SANITIZED: _____

ATP SCORE: _____ **PASSING SCORE:** Y   N

ADDRESS: _____

CITY, ST, ZIP: _____

CERTIFIED PROFESSIONAL

MOLD, ODOR, GERM & BACTERIA FREE

Nobody cares how much you know,
until they know how much you care.

During the past five years of research, testing, and doing the wax-on- wax-off work required to become a professional in my field, it has been an amazing personal transformation.

I have had the privilege of helping hundreds solve issues that were disrupting their health and life. Regardless of issue; mold, odor, allergy or returning a toxic environment to non-toxic, nothing has equaled the immense satisfaction of knowing I helped.

I charge for my work, so I'm not seeking sainthood or an atta boy upon entering the pearly gates. (I gave up expecting that greeting long ago!).

One of my first Realtor referrals came from a young man whose wife was in the hospital. His voice broke while explaining the tremendous stress he was experiencing while caring for their two small children and desperately wanting/needing to be there for his wife.

I was in the middle of treating a Hurricane Harvey flooded home. I stopped and walked to the backyard and sat under a tree. I related to him the familiarity of being in that position myself, several years prior.

His wife's health issue began shortly after moving into their older home. I asked many questions, all red flags pointed to toxic mold. He asked, "How much will it cost to treat my home? I have to confess, I'm flat broke."

I asked, "How much is your family's health worth to you?" He went silent. I said, "I can't place a value on it either."

AUTHOR BIO

E dward Kampf is the founder of Hygienitech Solutions, LL. He is one of the leading experts in deodorizing and decontamination in the Texas market.

Though he had a career as a mortgage banker, Ed's journey into indoor decontamination began after his daughter developed a rash from Dust Mite exposure at a hotel. That started his research into the toxicity of indoor environments, which quickly became a new passion. He left his other career and created a company based on the concept of creating healthy homes by treating toxic environments with non-toxic solutions. His discoveries are eye-opening as well as body-cleansing.

Edward Kampf's two-hour Texas Realtor CE course, "Staying Healthy in an Unhealthy Environment," has rapidly placed him in high demand on the speaking circuit. He currently resides in Houston, Texas.

Made in the USA
Columbia, SC
22 April 2025

56883615R00057